DEEPSEEK: THE DISRUPTIVE FORCE IN AI

How a Chinese AI Model is Challenging Silicon Valley

Farouk Mezghich
Linktr.ee/farkao/

Abstract:

Artificial intelligence has long been dominated by a handful of powerful Silicon Valley giants—Open AI, Google, and Meta—who have shaped the industry with closed-source models, billion-dollar training budgets, and proprietary AI systems. However, a new disruptive force has emerged from China, shaking the very foundations of AI development.

Deepseek is not just another AI model—it is a radical redefinition of how AI can be built, trained, and distributed. Developed by a research team linked to the High Flyer Quant hedge fund, Deepseek has achieved state-of-the-art AI performance at a fraction of the cost of its Western counterparts. Trained on a budget of just $5.6 million, Deepseek's models, Deepseek-V3 and Deepseek-R1, rival Open AI's GPT-4 while being fully open-source and 10x cheaper to use.

This book explores Deepseek's origins, technical breakthroughs, and geopolitical implications, shedding light on how China bypassed U.S. semiconductor restrictions, how the AI industry reacted with trillions lost in market value, and how Deepseek is democratizing AI by making high-performance models available for free.

As AI development moves toward open-source innovation, Deepseek represents a pivotal moment in the AI arms race, challenging the business models of Big Tech while enabling developers, researchers, and startups to build powerful AI applications without gatekeepers.

- Will proprietary AI models like GPT-4 survive in an open-source world?

- Can Silicon Valley maintain its AI dominance, or has China caught up?

- Is this the beginning of a fully democratized AI future?

Deepseek is not just another AI—it is a paradigm shift that redefines the future of artificial intelligence. This book provides an in-depth analysis of its impact, offering insights for AI enthusiasts, developers, investors, and policymakers who want to understand the next wave of AI disruption.

Welcome to the future of AI.

TABLE OF CONTENTS

Introduction

What is Deepseek?

In an industry dominated by a handful of Silicon Valley giants, a new player has emerged from an unexpected corner of the world— China. Deepseek AI, a revolutionary open-source large language model (LLM), has made headlines not just for its technical prowess but also for its staggering cost efficiency. Developed by a Chinese research lab linked to High Flyer Quant, a hedge fund managing $8 billion in assets, Deepseek has sent shockwaves through the AI industry by proving that state-of-the-art AI models do not require billions of dollars to develop.

Deepseek's V3 and R1 models have outperformed or matched leading Western AI models, including OpenAI's GPT-4, Meta's Llama, and Anthropic's Claude, all while being trained on a budget of only $5.6 million—a fraction of the billions spent by American tech companies.

Why is it Significant?

Deepseek represents a radical shift in AI development. Up until now, AI has been monopolized by a few elite companies—OpenAI, Google, Meta, and Anthropic—who have spent years and billions of dollars refining their models while keeping their architectures tightly closed. These companies have positioned themselves as the gatekeepers of advanced AI, charging high fees for API access and controlling how their models are used.

Deepseek changes this narrative by embracing open-source AI, democratizing access to cutting-edge technology and challenging Silicon Valley's closed-source dominance. For the first time, high-performing AI models are available to developers, researchers, and startups worldwide, allowing them to build applications without relying on expensive, proprietary models**.

The Context of AI Development:

To understand the impact of Deepseek, it's essential to explore the broader context of AI evolution:

The Dominance of Silicon Valley:

- AI has been largely controlled by OpenAI, Google, Meta, and Anthropic, each vying to build the most powerful language models. Their models, such as GPT-4 and Gemini, are trained using vast amounts of computational power, often requiring 100,000+GPUsandmulti-billion-dollar budgets**.

The Cost& Complexity of Training AI Models:

- AI training is an extraordinarily expensive process. OpenAI alone spends over $5 billion annually, while Google expects to spend$50billiononAIinfrastructurein2024. Deepseek,on the other hand, has demonstrated that AI models can be trained for less than $6 million, using more efficient algorithms and hardware**.

The Shift Toward Open-Source AI:

- While OpenAI has kept its technology closed, Meta's Llama models have pioneered an open-source approach, allowing researchers to modify and experiment with AI models freely. Deepseek has taken this a step further, releasing fully transparent training details, architectures, and codebases. This has allowed developers worldwide to run Deepseek models locally, bypassing the restrictions imposed by proprietary AI providers**.

What's at Stake?

Deepseek's emergence has caused a major disruption, sparking debates about national security, economic dominance, and AI ethics. The U.S. government has long imposed semiconductor restrictions to slow China's AI progress, but Deepseek has found ways to train competitive models with NVIDIA's less powerful H800 GPUs, effectively bypassing these constraints**.

Beyond geopolitics, Deepseek has the potential to democratize AI by significantly reducing costs for developers and businesses. For instance, Deepseek's API costs just $0.10 per million tokens, compared to OpenAI's $4.40 per million tokens—a 97% cost reduction that could shift AI development away from Silicon Valley**.

This book will explore how Deepseek was built, how it works, and why it has the potential to change AI forever.

01

The Birth of Deepseek

> **"**
>
> Deepseek was developed by a Chinese research lab linked to High Flyer Quant and has shocked the AI world by achieving performance parity with models like GPT-4 at a cost of just $5.6 million.
>
> Unlike OpenAI's closed-source approach, Deepseek embraces open-source AI, making advanced models available to developers worldwide.
>
> **"**

Origins & Background:

In a world where artificial intelligence has largely been developed by American tech giants, Deepseek emerged from an unexpected place —China. Unlike OpenAI, Google, and Meta, which have spent billions on AI research, Deepseek was developed by a relatively unknown Chinese research lab linked to High Flyer Quant, a hedge fund managing approximately $8 billion in assets**.

What makes Deepseek even more intriguing is the secrecy surrounding its development. Unlike OpenAI, which has a well-documented leadership team including Sam Altman and Ilya Sutskever, little is known about Deepseek's founder. Chinese media reports indicate that the lab was led by Liang Wenfeng, but beyond that, no detailed information exists on its leadership, funding sources, or early team members**.

What makes Deepseek even more intriguing is the secrecy surrounding its development. Unlike OpenAI, which has a well-documented leadership team including Sam Altman and Ilya Sutskever, little is known about Deepseek's founder. Chinese media reports indicate that the lab was led by Liang Wenfeng, but beyond that, no detailed information exists on its leadership, funding sources, or early team members**.

The Speed & Cost of Development:

Deepseek's rapid rise defies conventional AI wisdom. In just **two months**, the team was able to train a model that competes directly with **GPT-4**, **Claude**, and Llama—all of which took years and billions of dollars to develop.

Deepseek's **cost efficiency is unprecedented:**

- **Deepseek R1 cost just $5.6 million** to train, compared to the $100+ million cost of training GPT-4.
- **It took only two months** to develop, compared to the years spent by Open AI and Google.
- **It runs on NVIDIA's less powerful H800 GPUs,** bypassing U.S. semiconductor restrictions**.

This raises important questions: How did Deepseek train such an advanced model so quickly? **How did they achieve such extreme cost savings?** The answer lies in their **architectural choices, training optimizations, and the power of open-source AI**.

The Open-Source vs Closed-Source War:

One of the most disruptive aspects of Deepseek is its commitment to **open-source AI**. Unlike OpenAI, which has gradually become **less transparent**, Deepseek has **fully released its model weights, code, and training details** for public use**.

Why Do OpenAI & Google Keep Their Models Closed?

The closed-source AI approach has dominated Silicon Valley for years. Companies like OpenAI argue that keeping models closed is necessary for safety, profitability, and competitive advantage. However, there are other key reasons why OpenAI, Google, and Anthropic have opted for closed AI models:

1.Monetization & Profitability – OpenAI charges $20/month for ChatGPT Plus, and API access costs $4.40 per million tokens. Keeping the model proprietary ensures revenue streams**.

2.Data Privacy & Security – Closed models prevent competitors from analyzing training data, which could include sensitive or proprietary information.

3.Regulatory & Ethical Concerns – OpenAI has stated that unrestricted AI models could be misused for disinformation, cybercrime, or military applications.

HowDeepseekChosetheOpen-Source Path:

Deepseek has **flipped the script** by going fully open-source. **Deepseek-R1 and Deepseek-V3** have been **released for free**, allowing developers worldwide to **download, modify, and run the models locally****.This means that any individual or company can now:

- **Run Deepseek AI models on their own hardware** without needing to pay OpenAI or Google.

- **Fine-tune models** for specific applications like customer service, legal research, or coding assistants.

- **Avoid censorship or usage restrictions** imposed by proprietary AI providers.

The result? **A massive shift toward decentralized AI development:**

Deepseek's API pricing is 10x cheaper than OpenAI, making it a more affordable option for developers and businesses. With a cost of just $0.10 per million tokens, developers can now build AI applications without breaking the bank**.

What This Means for AI Research &Innovation:

Deepseek's open-source approach is a direct challenge to OpenAI's monopoly. While OpenAI has relied on secrecy and billion-dollar investments, Deepseek has demonstrated that AI models can be built quickly, efficiently, and cheaply.

This has led to panic in Silicon Valley. Industry leaders, including former Google CEO Eric Schmidt, have acknowledged that China has "caught up" in AI within just six months**.

Investors and researchers are now rethinking the future of AI development, questioning whether closed-source AI is sustainable in a world where powerful models are freely available.

Conclusion:

Deepseek's rapid development and open-source philosophy have changed the game. By proving that state-of-the-art AI can be trained on a budget, Deepseek has sparked a new wave of AI democratization.

Understanding Deepseek Models

> 66
>
> Deepseek's flagship models, Deepseek-V3 and Deepseek-R1, introduce groundbreaking efficiencies in AI training.
>
> By leveraging techniques like Mixture of Experts (MoE) and Chain of Thought Reasoning, Deepseek competes with top AI models at a fraction of the cost.
>
> 99

Deepseek-V3 vs. Deepseek-R1: Breaking Down the Models:

Deepseek AI has released **two primary models: Deepseek-V3** and **Deepseek-R1**. While both models are state-of-the-art, they serve different purposes and introduce groundbreaking advancements in AI efficiency, performance, and cost reduction.

Deepseek-V3: The Flagship Model:

Deepseek-V3 is comparable to OpenAI's GPT-4 and Meta's Llama 3 **in terms of raw performance.** It is a large-scale transformer model trained on a vast corpus of text **and optimized for general-purpose AI tasks.**

Key Features of Deepseek-V3:

- **General-Purpose AI Model:** Capable of handling text generation, conversation, summarization, coding, and logical reasoning tasks.

- **High Efficiency:** Trained for just $5.6 million, compared to the $100+ million it cost to train GPT-4**.

- **API-Accessible & Open-Source:** Unlike GPT-4, which is closed and proprietary, Deepseek-V3 is freely available for developers to use, fine-tune, and run locally.

- **Performance Parity with GPT-4:** Benchmarks show that Deepseek-V3 matches or outperforms OpenAI's models on several tasks**.

Deepseek-R1:TheNext-GenerationReasoning Model:

Deepseek-R1 is an **advanced AI reasoning model** that directly competes with Open AI's **GPT-4o**. It was designed to enhance **logical thinking, multi-step reasoning, and problem-solving capabilities**.

Key Features of Deepseek-R1:

- **Chain of Thought Reasoning (CoT):** Unlike traditional AI models that generate one-off answers, **Deepseek-R1 can think step-by-step**, improving accuracy on complex problems.

- **Self-Generated Reasoning Paths:** Instead of relying on massive labeled datasets, Deepseek-R1 trains itself to reason through problems,drasticallyreducingtraining costs**.

- **Open-Source & Transparent:** Unlike OpenAI's **O1 model**, which also uses reasoning steps but remains closed-source, Deepseek- R1is fully **accessible fordevelopers andresearchers**.

- **Superior Mathematical & Coding Performance:** Benchmarks showDeepseek-R1outperformsGPT-4 **and Claude in math and coding tasks**, particularly in multi-step logic**.

Performance Comparison: Deepseek vs. GPT-4, Claude, and Llama:

Benchmark Results:

Deepseek's models have been rigorously tested against OpenAI's GPT-4, Meta's Llama 3, and Anthropic's Claude. The results have stunned the AI community, showing that Deepseek performs at near-parity with the best models on the market—despite being trained on a fraction of the budget.

AI Model	Math & Logic Performance	Code Generation	General Reasoning	Training Cost
GPT-4o	(High)	(Best)	(Best)	$100M+
Claude 3.5	(High)	(Very High)	(Very High)	$50M+
Llama 3	(Medium)	(Medium)	(Medium)	$30M+
Deepseek-V3	(High)	(Very High)	(Very High)	$5.6M
Deepseek-R1	(Best)	(Best)	(Best)	$5.6M

Key Takeaways:

✔ Deepseek-R1beatsGPT-4oinreasoning andcoding,especially in math-heavy tasks.

✔ Deepseek-V3matchesGPT-4butcosts 20x less to train.

✔ OpenAI and Anthropic still have an edge in general language fluency, but Deepseek is closing the gap.

✔ Meta'sLlama3lagsbehindDeepseek,despitebeing open-source.

Break through Features of Deepseek Models:

Deepseek's cost and **efficiency advantages** come from several key innovations in AI training and model architecture. These features not only reduce computational expenses but also e**nhance performance, making AI more accessible**.

1. Mixture of Experts (MoE) – Optimized Computation:

Traditional AI models like GPT-4 process every query using the entire neural network, which is expensive and inefficient. Deepseek, however, uses a technique called Mixture of Experts (MoE).

◆ **How It Works:**

Instead of activating the entire model, **MoE activates only the necessary parts** based on the type of question asked. For example:

- If you ask a **math question**, only the math-related neurons are activated. If you ask a **coding question**, only the coding-related neurons are used.

Benefits:

✔ Uses only 30% of the model's parameters per query, cutting computational costs dramatically.

✔ Runsmoreefficientlyonconsumer hardware.

✔ Allows Deepseek models to be as powerful as GPT-4, but at a fraction of the cost.

2.Chain of Thought Reasoning–Enhancing AI Logic:

Unlike traditional AI models that produce **one-shot answers**, Deepseek-R1 **thinks step-by-step** like a human would when solving aproblem.

How It Works:

- Instead of jumping to an answer, Deepseek **writes down its reasoning process** before reaching a conclusion. This approach
- **improves accuracy in complex problem-solving**, especially in math and logic.

Benefits:

- ✓ Moreaccurateproblem-solving,especially in math and physics.

- ✓ Better debugging and code analysis.

- ✓ Improves transparency—users can see how the AI arrived at an answer.

3.Distillation Technique–Making Smaller Models Powerful:

Deepseek uses a technique called **distillation**, where a **large AI model is used to train a smaller one**. This allows Deepseek to **compress knowledge into a smaller**, **more efficient model** without losing much accuracy.

How It Works:

A **large teacher model** (e.g., Deepseek-V3) is used to generate high-quality training data. A **smaller model (e.g., Deepseek-R1)** is then trained on this data to replicate the larger model's intelligence.

Benefits:

- ✓ AllowsDeepseektorunefficientlyon lower-end GPUs.

- ✓ Reduces the need for massive datasets.

- ✓ Enables smaller businesses and researchers to run powerful AI locally.

4. Efficient Training –The $5.6 Million AI Revolution:

Deepseek's biggest shock to Silicon Valley was its ability to train a world-class AI model for just $5.6 million.

How It Works:

- Instead of training on **hundreds of thousands of GPUs, Deepseek optimized its training pipeline** using:

    - **Smaller, high-quality datasets**   (rather than scraping the entire internet).

    - **Mathematical optimizations** to reduce computational costs.

    - **Lower-power NVIDIA H800 GPUs,** avoiding reliance on U.S.-banned H100 chips.

Results:

✓ MassivecostreductioninAItraining(20x cheaper than GPT-4).

✓ Provesthatbillion-dollarbudgetsarenotnecessary forcutting-edge AI.

Conclusion:

Deepseek's **game-changing AI models** are proving that **AI development does not have to be an exclusive club**. By leveraging **MixtureofExperts, ChainofThoughtReasoning, and Distillation**, Deepseek has built a model that competes with the best, at a fraction of the cost.

In the next chapter, we'll dive into **Deepseek's hardware and cost efficiency**, revealing how China bypassed U.S. semiconductor restrictionsandstillbuiltaworld-class AI.

CHAPTER

Deepseek's Hardware & Cost Efficiency

> **"**
>
> Unlike OpenAI and Google, which spend billions on AI infrastructure, Deepseek optimized its model training, relying on cheaper NVIDIA H800 GPUs and efficient computation techniques to lower costs significantly.
>
> **"**

How Much Does It Cost to Train an AI?

For years, **AI development has been a game of big budget sand massive computing power.** Companies like OpenAI, Google, and Meta have spent billions on **data centers, GPU clusters, and energy costs** to train their AI models.

Here'sabreakdownofthestaggeringcosts behind leadinAI models:

AI Model	Training Cost	GPUs Used	Electricity& DataCosts
GPT-4	$100M+	10,000+H100 GPUs	Extremelyhigh
Claude3.5	$50M+	8,000+ GPUs	Veryhigh
Llama 3	$30M+	6,000+ GPUs	High
Deepseek-V3	$5.6M	~1,500GPUs	Minimal

Why AI Training is So Expensive?

- **Hardware Costs:** AI models require thousands of high-end **NVIDIA H100orA100GPUs,** which cost **$30,000+perunit.**

- **Electricity & Cooling:** Training AI consumes **massive amounts of electricity,** requiring **dedicated power plants** in some cases.

- **Data Costs:** AI training relies on scraping and processing trillions of words, requiring **high-bandwidth data centers.**

How Deepseek Slashed Training Costs?

Deepseek **broke the traditional AI training model** by using **innovative hardware and software techniques** to keep costs low.

✔ Trained using NVIDIA's H800 GPUs (cheaper & less powerful than H100s).

✓ Used smaller, higher-quality data sets instead of scraping the entire internet.

✓ Applied advanced optimization reduce energy consumption.

✓ Leveraged Mixture of Experts (MoE) to lower computational requirements.

The Hardware Used to Run Deepseek Locally:

One of Deepseek's most impressive features is that it can be **run locally** on consumer hardware—something impossible for GPT-4 or Claude.

Here's what you need to run Deepseek AI on your own system:

Deepseek's Recommended Hardware Setup:

Component	Recommended Specs	Cost as January 2025
Motherboard	Gigabyte MZ73 (or equivalent)	$1,500
CPU	2x AMD EPYC (High-core count	$1,700
RAM	24x DDR5 (32GB or more)	$4,800
GPU (optional)	NVIDIA H800 or RTX 4090	
Storage	NVMe SSD (1TB+)	$75

Why This Matters: Unlike Open AI's models, which require **cloud access and expensive API fees, Deepseek can run on-premises, giving businesses full control over their AI models.**

Key Benefits:

✓ No need to pay OpenAI for API access.

✓ Privacy & security—data stays local.

✓ Lowerlong-termcostscomparedtocloud-based AI models.

How China Bypassed U.S. Chip Restrictions & Still Built Efficient and AI?

One of the biggest challenges facing Chinese AI companies has been **U.S. semiconductor restrictions**, which prevent access to **NVIDIA' some of powerful AI chips(H100 &A100 GPUs).**

How Deepseek Worked Around These Restrictions?

🔲 **Used NVIDIA H800 GPUs: A weaker but still capable** version of theH100,whichtheU.S.stillallowsChina to purchase.

🔲 **Optimized Software & Training Techniques:** By **cutting unnecessary computations, Deepseek was able to get H800 GPUs to perform at near-H100 levels.**

✅ **Leveraged Distributed Training:** Deepseek used **multiple lower-power GPUs working together**, instead of relying on a single ultra-powerful chip.

Result: Deepseek achieved world-class AI performance without relying on banned U.S. technology.

Why Deepseek's Cost Efficiency is a Game-Changer?

Deepseek has proven that **cutting-edge AI does not require billions of dollars to develop.** This could have major **long-term effects** on the AI industry:

- **Lower Barriers to Entry** – Startups and independent researchers cannowbuildAImodelswithoutrequiring massive VC funding.

- **Open-Source Revolution** – If Deepseek's model continues to succeed, other companies may be forced to lower their costs or go open-source to compete.

- **Threat to Big Tech's AI Monopoly** – Open AI, Google, and Meta may struggle to justify their **high-cost, closed-source AI models** when Deepseekisfreelyavailableatafraction of the price.

Conclusion:

Deepseek's efficient hardware and cost-saving strategies have **shattered the AI industry's traditional cost barriers. By proving that high-performance AI can be built with just$5.6M, Deepseek has challenged the dominance of billion-dollar AI corporations.**

In the next chapter, we'll explore the **impact of Deepseek on Silicon Valley,thes tock market, and global AI competition.**

The Deepseek Shockwave in the AI Industry

66

Deepseek's rise has sent shockwaves through Silicon Valley, challenging OpenAI's monopoly and even affecting stock market valuations, with billions lost in response to its disruptive entry into the AI space.

99

Impact on Silicon Valley & Big Tech:

The release of Deepseek has **sent shock waves through Silicon Valley**, forcing major AI players to **rethink their strategies**. Until now, the AI industry has been **dominated by a handful of powerful companies** — OpenAI, Google, Meta, and Anthropic—who have relied on **closed-source AI models, high training costs, and premium-priced APIs**.

Deepseek's **high-performance, open-source, and low-cost** approach has changed the game overnight.

Stock Market Reactions: A $1 Trillion Disruption:

The financial world quickly **reacted to Deepseek's emergence**, with some of the biggest AI companies **losing billions in market value** almost instantly.

✓ **NVIDIA Stock Dropped Sharply – Investors fear that AI efficiency break throughs** could reduce demand for NVIDIA's high-end GPUs, which are currently essential for AI training**.

✓ **Microsoft & OpenAI Investors Worry – Microsoft has invested $13 billion into OpenAI**, but with Deepseek offering a **similar performance for a fraction of the cost, its business model is now under threat**.

✓ **Meta's Llama Models Face a New Competitor – Meta has been pushing open-source AI** with Llama 3, but Deepseek's performance **surpassed Llama at a lower cost**, making it the new go-to open-source model.

Total Estimated Market Losses from Deepseek's Announcement: Over $620 billion in one day.**

How Deepseek Challenges the Open AI Monopoly:

For years, **Open AI has controlled access to cutting-edge AI** by:

✓ Keeping GPT-4 closed-source

✓ Charging high prices for API access

✓ RequiringbusinessestodependonOpenAI's cloud

Deepseek's Disruptive Advantages:

- **Open-Source Availability:** Anyone can download, modify, and run Deepseek locally.
- **10x Cheaper API Pricing:** Open AI charges **$4.40 per million tokens, while Deepseek only costs $0.10per million tokens**.**
- **Runs Locally on Consumer Hardware:** Unlike GPT-4, which requires cloud access, Deepseek models can be run on personal GPUs.

The Result: Many **developers, startups, and even large corporations are now switching to Deepseek instead of paying Open AI.**

Geo political & Strategic Implications:

US Chip Bans & China's Workarounds:

The **U.S. has imposed strict semi conductor export control son China**, aiming to **limit China's AI progress** by restricting access to **high-end NVIDIA H100 GPUs**. However, Deepseek has demonstrated that **China no longer needs access to banned chips to compete with the West**.

✓ **Trained on NVIDIA H800s** – Weaker than H100s but still effective

✓ **Advanced Software Optimizations** – Achieved **high efficiency without cutting-edge chips**

✓ **Distributed Computing** – Used **multiple cheaper GPUs** instead of relying on expensive high-end models

Implication: China has now caught up in AI without needing direct access to America's most powerful GPUs.

The AI Arms Race: A Level Playing Field:

For years, the **U.S. was thought to be 2-3 years ahead of China** in AI development. However, according to former **Google CEO Eric Schmidt,** , China has **closed the gap within six months**, largely due to Deepseek**.

✓ **U.S. thought AI dominance was secured**–The rapid success of Deepseek proves otherwise.

✓ **Open-source AI is accelerating global competition** – If Deepseek succeeds, other nations may adopt similar strategies.

✓ **AI development is shifting away from billion-dollar monopolies** – Smaller teams with efficient techniques can now compete with tech giants.

The Result: The **global AI race is no longer just about money and hardware—it's** about efficiency, open-source innovation, and accessibility.

What Does This Mean for the Future of AI?

Deepseek's success **raises serious questions** about the **future of AI development:**

1- Will AI Become Fully Democratized?

Deep seek has **proven that state-of-the-art AI can be built on a budget.** If this trend continues:

✓ More AI models will become open-source

✓ Startupscancompetewithoutneeding billions in funding

✓ Developers will have more control over AI systems

2- Will Closed-Source AI Die Out?

Big Tech companies argue that **keeping AI models closed is necessary for safety and profit ability.** However, if **Deepseek proves that open-source models can thrive,** companies like Open AI **may be forced to re think their approach.**

3-Will China Lead the Next Wave of AI Innovation?

Deepseek's **break through in AI efficiency** suggests that China **may have an advantage in future AI developments**. If China continues this **cost-effective, open-source strategy**, it could **surpass the U.S. in AI dominance** within the next few years.

The Takeaway: The AI industry is at a turning point. **The days of billion-dollar AI monopolies maybe over.**

Conclusion:

Deepseek has **shaken the AI industry to its core**, proving that **high-performance AI no longer requires billions of dollars or proprietary restrictions**.

In the next chapter, we'll explore **how developers and businesses can start using Deepseek today—via API access and local deployments**.

05

Running Deepseek Locally

"

One of Deepseek's biggest advantages is that it can run locally, reducing dependency on expensive cloud services. This chapter provides guidance on using the Deepseek API and deploying models on personal hardware.

"

Using Deepseek via API:

One of Deepseek's biggest advantages over proprietary models like Open AI's GPT-4 is its **low-cost, developer-friendly API.** While Open AI charges **$4.40 per million tokens,** Deepseek's **API** costs only **$0.10per million tokens—a 97%cost reduction**.

How Developers Can Integrate Deepseek into Applications?

For businesses and developers looking to use Deepseek in applications such as **chatbots, coding assistants, or AI-powered analytics**, the API offers an easy and scalable solution.

Step 1: Access Deepseek's API

- Visit Deepseek's official documentation page.
- Obtain an API key by signing up for access.

Step 2: Install Required Libraries

To interact with Deepseek's API, you'll need Python and HTTP request handling.

```python
-Python

importrequests

API_KEY = "your_deepseek_api_key"

url = "https://api.deepseek.com/v1/chat"

payload = {
"model": "deepseek-v3",
"messages":[{"role":"user","content": "What is Deepseek?"}]

headers={
"Authorization": f"Bearer {API_KEY}",
"Content-Type": "application/json"
```

```
response=requests.post(url,json=payload, headers=headers)
print(response.json())
```

Step 3: Adjust API Parameters

The API supports features like:

- **Temperature Control:** Adjust response randomness (0.1 for precise, 0.9 for creative). **Max Tokens:** Set response length limits.

Fine-tuning Options: Customize the model for specific tasks

Pricing Comparison: Deepseek vs. OpenAI:

AI Provider	Cost per Million Tokens
Deepseek	$0.10
OpenAI GPT-4o	$4.40
Anthropic Claude	$3.00
Meta Llama 3	$0.20

📌 **Result:** Businesses can now build AI applications at a fraction of the cost, allowing startups and enterprises alike to scale without heavy expenses.

Running Deepseek on Personal Hardware:

One of Deepseek's most powerful features is its **ability to run locally,** making it **independent of cloud services** like OpenAI's API. This is particularly useful for:

✓ Developers who want full control over AI models.

✓ Businessesconcernedaboutdataprivacy and security.

✓ AI researchers who need to fine-tune models on specific datasets.

Deepseek Models Available for Download:

Deepseek provides downloadable weights for **Deepseek-V3 and R1,** which can be run on personal hardware.

Hardware Requirements:

Component	Recommended Specs
CPU	AMDEPYC/IntelXeon
RAM	128GBDDR5 (Minimum 64GB)
GPU	NVIDIA RTX 4090 / A100 / H800
Storage	2TB+ NVMe SSD

Running Deepseek on Personal Hardware:

One of Deepseek's most powerful features is its **ability to run locally,** making it **independent of cloud services** like OpenAI's API. This is particularly useful for:

✔ Developers who want full control over AI models.

✔ Businesses concerned about data privacy and security.

✔ AI researchers who need to fine-tune models on specific data sets.

Deepseek Models Available for Download:

Deepseek provides downloadable weights for **Deepseek-V3 and R1,** which can be run on personal hardware.

Hardware Requirements:

Component	Recommended Specs
CPU	AMDEPYC/IntelXeon
RAM	128GBDDR5 (Minimum 64GB)
GPU	NVIDIA RTX 4090 / A100 / H800
Storage	2TB+ NVMe SSD

How to Run Deepseek Locally:

Step 1: Install Dependencies

Ensure you have **Python, PyTorch, and Hugging Face Transformers** installed.

Bash
pip install torch transformers accelerate

Step 2: Download Deepseek Model Weights

Python

```python
from transformers import AutoModelForCausal
LM, AutoTokenizer

model_name = "deepseek-ai/deepseek-v3"
tokenizer=AutoTokenizer.from_pretrained(model_name)
model=AutoModelForCausalLM.from_pretrained(model_name)
inputs=tokenizer("Explain Deepseek AI.", return_tensors="pt")
outputs =model.generate(**inputs, max_length=200)
print(tokenizer.decode(outputs[0]))
```

Step 3: Optimize for Low-End GPUs

✓

If using consumer GPUs, enable8-bit precision for reduced VRAM usage.

```
Python

from transformers import BitsAndBytesConfigquantization_
config BitsAndBytesConfig (load_in_8bit=True)

model = AutoModelForCausalLM.from_pretrained(model_name,
quantization_config=quantization_config)
```

Result: Developers can now **run AI locally without relying on Open AI, Google, or Microsoft, ensuring lower costs and full data privacy.**

Challenges & Solutions When Running AI Locally:

1. Hardware Limitations:

Problem: Many consumer-grade GPUs may **struggle with large models**.

Solution: Use **quantized versions (8-bit or 4-bit models)** to reduce VRAM usage.

2. Storage & Memory Bottlenecks:

Problem: AI models require large amountsof **RAM & diskspace**.

✓ **Solution:** Use **NVMe SSDs** for faster model loading and **increase swap memory.**

3. Model Fine-Tuning for Specific Use Cases:

Problem: Default models may not perform well on niche datasets.

✔ **Solution:** Use **LoRA (Low-Rank Adaptation) fine-tuning** to train models efficiently.

Python
frompeftimportLoraConfiglora_config ╪LoraConfig ╷ *r=8, lora_alpha=16, lora_dropout=0.05)*

The Takeaway: Running Deepseek locally is possible with hard ware optimizations, fine-tuning techniques, and proper resource management.

Conclusion:

Deepseek offers **unparalleled flexibility**—whether through its **cheap API pricing or its ability to run on personal hardware**. This makes it the **most accessible state-of-the-art AI model available today**, democratizing AI for **developers, businesses, and researchers worldwide**.

In the next chapter, we'll explore **what the future holds for Deepseek and how it could re define AI development in the coming years**.

CHAPTER

06

Deploying Deepseek R1 on Microsoft Azure

Deploying Deepseek R1 on Microsoft Azure Machine Learning's Managed Online Endpoints enables scalable, secure, and efficient AI inference. This chapter outlines the step-by-step process to set up and deploy Deepseek R1 using Azure's infrastructure while ensuring low latency, high availability, and cost efficiency.

In this chapter, we explore the process of deploying DeepseekR1 on Microsoft Azure using Azure Machine Learning's Managed Online Endpoints. This approach ensures efficient, scalable, and secure real-time inference, granting full control over data within your Azure subscription. By deploying DeepseekR1ina region of your choice, you can comply with regional data governance requirements.

Tools and Technologies Utilized:

- vLLM: A high-throughput and memory-efficient inference and serving engine designed for large language models (LLMs). vLLM optimizes model execution through advanced memory management techniques, enabling continuous batching of incoming requests and rapid processing. It supports seamless integration with Hugging Face models and offers various decoding algorithms, including parallel sampling and beam search. Additionally, vLLM supports tensor and pipeline parallel ism for distributed inference, making it a flexible solution for LLM deployment.

- Azure Machine Learning Managed Online Endpoints: These endpoints provide a streamlined and scalable method to deploy machine learning models for real-time inference. They handle the complexities of serving, scaling, securing, and monitoring models, allowing developers to focus on model development without the burden of infrastructure management.

Deployment Steps:

1. **Create a Custom Environment for vLLM on AzureML:**

   - **Dockerfile Creation:** Begin by creating a Dockerfile that defines the environment for the model. Utilize vLLM's base container, which includes all necessary dependencies and drivers:

```
Dockerfile

FROM vllm/vllm-openai:latest
ENV MODEL_NAME deepseek-ai/DeepSeek-R1-Distill-Llama-8B

ENTRYPOINT python3 -m vllm.entrypoints.openai.api_server --
model$ MODEL_NAME$ VLLM_ARGS
```

This setup allows for flexibility in defining which model to deploy during deployment time by passing them odeln'-amevia an environment variable.

- **Azure ML Work space Configuration: Log into your Azure Machine Learning workspace:**

```
Bash

azaccountset--subscription<subscription ID>

azconfigure--defaultsworkspace=<Azure Machine
Learning workspace name>group=<resourcegroup>
```

- ***Environment Definition:*** *Create an environment. yml file to specify the environment settings:*

Yaml

```
$schema:https://azuremlschemas.azureedge.net/latest/environment.
schema.json name: r1

build:
path: . dockerfile_path: Dockerfile
```

- o **Endpoint Creation: Deploy the endpoint:**

Bash

```
az ml online-endpoint create -f endpoint.yml
```

- o **Docker Image Retrieval:** Obtain the Docker image address from Azure ML Studio under Environments ->r1.

- o **Deployment Configuration:** Create a deployment.yml file to configure the deployment settings and display the desired model from Hugging Face via vLLM:

Yaml

```yaml
$schema:
  https://azuremlschemas.azureedge.net/latest/managedOnline
  Deployment.schema.json

name: current
endpoint_name: r1-prod
environment_variables:
MODEL_NAME: deepseek-ai/DeepSeek-R1-Distill-Llama-8B
VLLM_ARGS:""#optionalargsforvLLM runtime
environment:
image: <Docker image address>
inference_config:

liveness_route:

port: 8000

path: /ping

readiness_route:

port: 8000
path: /health
scoring_route:
port: 8000
path: /
instance_type: Standard_NC24ads_A100_v4
```

```
instance_count: 1
request_settings:
max_concurrent_requests_per_instance: 32
request_timeout_ms: 60000
liveness_probe:
initial_delay: 10
period: 10


timeout: 2 success_threshold: 1


failure_threshold: 30
readiness_probe:
initial_delay:      120
period: 10 timeout: 2
success_threshold:   1
failure_threshold: 30

'
```

Parameter Considerations:

- **instance_count:** Defines the number of nodes to deploy.

- **max_concurrent_requests_per_instance:** Sets the number ofconcurrentrequestsallowedbeforereturning an HTTP 429 error.

- **request_timeout_ms:** Specifies the duration (in milliseconds) before the endpoint closes the connection, returning an HTTP 408 error if exceeded.

Impact of Parameter Adjustments:

- Increasing max_concurrent_requests_per_instance can enhanceoverallthroughputbutmay increaselatency for individual calls.

- Adjusting request_timeout_ms allows clients to wait longer for a response, provided the concurrent request limit is not exceeded.

- Modifying instance_count scales throughput and cost linearly.

o   Model v Deployment: Deploy the Deepseek R1 model:

Bash
*azmlonline-deploymentcreate-fdeployment.yml --all-traffi*ı

3. Testing the Deployment:

Testing the Deployment:

After successfully deploying DeepseekR1 on Azure Machine Learning's Managed Online Endpoints, it's essential to verify that the model is functioning as expected. Here's how you can test your deployment:

1. **Retrieve EndpointDetails:**

- ○ **Scoring URI:** This is the URL where your model is hosted and can be accessed for inference.

- ○ **APIKeys:**Thesekeysarenecessaryforauthenticating your requests to the endpoint.

Youcanobtainthesedetailsusingthe Azure CLI:

Bash
az ml online-endpoint show -n r1-prod azmlonline-endpointget-credentials-n r1-prod

- **Environment Definition:** Create an environment. yml file to specify the environment settings:

Yaml
$schema: https://azuremlschemas.azureedge.net/latest/ environment. schema.json name: r1 build:

Path:
dockerfile_path: Dockerfile

- **Environment Build:** Build the environment using the Azure CLI:

Bash
az ml environment create -f environment.yml

1. **Deploy the Azure ML Managed Online Endpoint:**

- **Endpoint Definition:** Create an endpoint.yml file to define the Managed Online Endpoint:

Yaml
$schema: *https://azuremlsdk2.blob.core.windows.net/latest/managedOnline Endpoint.schema.json* *name: r1-prod auth_mode: key*

- ***Endpoint Creation:*** *Deploy the endpoint:*

Bash
az ml online-endpoint create -f endpoint.yml

- **Docker Image Retrieval:** Obtain the Docker image address from AzureML Studio under Environments ->r1.

- **Deployment Configuration:** Create a deployment.yml file to configure the deployment settings and deploy the desired model from Hugging Face via vLLM:

Yaml

```
schema:
https://azuremlschemas.azureedge.net/latest/managedOnline
Deployment.schema.json
name: current
endpoint_name: r1-prod
environment_variables:
MODEL_NAME: deepseek-ai/DeepSeek-R1-Distill-Llama-8B
VLLM_ARGS:""#optionalargsfor vLLM runtime
environment:
image: <Docker image address>
inference_config:
liveness_route:
port: 8000

path: /
instance_type:Standard_NC24ads_A100_v4 instance_count: 1
request_settings: max_concurrent_requests_per_instance:
32 request_timeout_ms: 60000
liveness_probe:
initial_delay: 10
```

```
period: 10
timeout: 2
success_threshold: 1

failure_threshold:30readiness_probe: initial_delay: 120

period: 10
timeout:2success_threshold:1failure_threshold: 30
```

Parameter Considerations:

- **instance_count:** Defines the number of nodes to deploy.

- **max_concurrent_requests_per_instance:** Sets the number of concurrent requests allowed before returning anHTTP429 error.

- **request_timeout_ms:** Specifies the duration (in milliseconds) before the end point closes the connection, returning an HTTP 408 error if exceeded.

Impact of Parameter Adjustments:

- Increasing max_concurrent_requests_per_instance can enhance over all through put but may increase latency for individual calls.

- Adjusting request_timeout_ms allows clients to wait longer for a response, provided the concurrent request limit is not exceeded.

- Modifying instance_count scales through put and cost linearly.

Model Deployment: Deploy the Deepseek R1 model:

```bash
Bash

azmlonline-deploymentcreate-fdeployment.yml --all-traffic)ı
```

3. Testing the Deployment:

Testing the Deployment:

After successfully deploying DeepseekR1 on Azure Machine Learning's Managed Online End points, it's essential to verify that the model is functioning as expected. Here's how you can test your deployment:

- **Retrieve Endpoint Details:**

  - **Scoring URI:** This is the URL where your model is hosted and can be accessed for inference.

  - **API Keys:** These keys are necessary for authenticating your requests to the endpoint.

You can obtain these details using the Azure CLI:

```bash
Bash

az mlonline-endpoint show-nr1-prod

azmlonline-endpointget-credentials-n r1-prod
```

2. Send a Test Request:

With the end point's scoring URI and API key in hand, you can send a test request to ensure the model is operational. Here's a Python code snippet to help you get started:

```python
import requests
#Replacewithyourendpoint'sscoring URI

url="https://r1prod<region>.inference.ml.azure.com/v1/chat/completions"

#ReplacewithyourAPIkeyheaders= {

"Content-Type": "application/json", "Authorization": "Bearer <your_api_key>"}

#Definetheinputpromptforthemodel data ={

"model":"deepseek-ai/DeepSeek-R1-Distill-Llama-8B", "messages": [
{
#Send the POST request totheendpoint
response=requests.post(url,headers=headers, json=data)
#Print the model's response
print(response.json())
```

Expected Output:

Upon executing the above code, you should receive a JSON response containing the model's answer to your prompt. For instance:

Json

```
{
  "id": "chatcmpl-xxxxxxxx-xxxx-xxxx-xxxx-xxxxxxxxxxxx",
  "object": "chat.completion",
  "created": 1738058980,
  "model":"deepseek-ai/DeepSeek-R1-Distill-Llama-8B","choices": [

  {
    "index": 0, "message": {

      role": "assistant",

"content":"DeployingAImodelsonAzure offers several
benefits,   includingscalableinfrastructure,robust security
features,andseamlessintegrationwithother Azure services."

    },
    "finish_reason": "stop"
  }
  ],
  "usage":{ "prompt_tokens": 11,
  "completion_tokens":42,"total_tokens": 53
  }
}
```

This response indicates that the model is correctly processing the input and generating appropriate outputs.

Monitoring the Deployment:

Once your model is up and running, it's crucial to monitor its performance to ensure it meets your application's requirements. Azureprovidestoolstohelpyoukeep an eye on various metrics:

- **Azure Monitor:** This service allows you to track resource utilization, including CPU and GPU usage, memory consumption, and more. By setting up alerts, you can pro actively manage potential issues before they impact your application's performance.

- **Logging:** Implement logging within your application to capture details about each inference request, such as response times, This information is in valuable for debugging and optimizing your model's performance. input parameters, and any errors encountered.

Autoscaling the Deployment:

To handle varying levels of demand efficiently, consider configuring auto scaling for your deployment. Azure Machine Learning's Managed Online End points support auto scaling based on predefined metrics and schedules

- **Metric-Based Scaling:** Set rules to scale out (add more instances) when metrics like CPU or GPU utilization exceed a certainthreshold.Conversely,scalein   (reduceinstances)when utilization drops below a specified level.

- **Schedule-Based Scaling:** Define scaling schedules based on expected usage patterns. For example, you might scale out during business hours when traffic is high and scale in during off-peak hours to save costs.

By implementing auto scaling, you ensure that your deployment remains responsive under load while optimizing resource usage and controlling costs.

Summary:

Deploying Deepseek R1 on Azure Machine Learning's Managed Online Endpoints provides a robust and scalable solution for real-time AI inference. By following the steps outlined above, you can set up, test, monitor, and scale your deployment effectively, ensuringoptimalperformanceandresource utilization.

For a detailed walkthrough and additional insights, refer to the original guide by Clemens Siebler.

CHAPTER

07

The Future Of AI After Deepseek

❝

Deepseek has proven that AI innovation does not require billion-dollar investments. Its success signals the rise of open-source AI, possibly leading to a decline in proprietary AI models.

❞

The Rise of Open-Source AI:

Deepseek's open-source release has reshaped the AI industry. Traditionally, AI innovation has been driven by closed-source, billion-dollar companies such as Open AI, Google, and Meta. However, Deepseek's success has proven that high-performance AI can be built efficiently and affordably, raising critical questions about the future of AI:

Will Open-Source AI Over take Proprietary Models?

With Deepseek and **Meta's Llama 3** leading the open-sourc movement, many experts believe that **closed-source AI may nolonger be sustainable**. Open-source models provide:

✓ **Lower costs** (free to use, no API fees)

✓ **Transparency** (developer scan inspect and modify the code)

✓ **Wider accessibility** (can be run locally or fine-tuned)

Prediction: In the next 3-5 years, open-source models may dominate AI, forcing proprietary models to either lower their prices or open up their architectures.

Will Open AI Be Forced to Change Its Business Model?

Open AI has relied on **monetizing closed-source models** like GPT-4 and GPT-4o. But with **Deepseek offering similar performance for 97% less cost**, developers are rapidly switching to **cheaper**, **open alternatives**.

If Deepseek continues to improve, Open AI may be forced to:

- **Release open-sourcemodels** (tostayrelevant)

- **Lower API costs significantly** (to compete with Deepseek's $0.10 per million tokens)

- **Shift focus from pure AI models to AI-powered applications**

Prediction: Open AI may transition into **offering enterprise AI solutions rather than just API access, similar to how Microsoft offers AI-powered business tools.**

What's Next for Deepseek?

Deepseek's first models have already shaken the AI industry, but **what comes next?**

1. Expansion Beyond Text Generation:

Currently, Deepseek focuses primarily on **language- based** AI (chatbots, coding, reasoning). However, future versions may expand into:

✔ **Multimodal AI** – Handling **text, images, and video together** like GPT-4o and Gemini.

✔ **AI Agents** – Models that can **autonomously execute tasks** (e.g., AI assistants that browse the web, send emails, or write reports).

✔ **AI-Generated Creativity** – Music, video generation, and advanced AI-generated media.

Prediction: By 2026, Deepseek could **introduce a multimodal model that competes with GPT-4o andGemini1.5.**

2.Improvements in Reasoning & Scientific AI:

Deepseek-R1 already **outperforms GPT-4 in logic-heavy tasks**, but the next frontier in AI development is **scientific AI**, including:

✔ **AI for Mathematics & Theoretical Science** – Helping researchers solve complex problems.

Prediction: Open AI may transition into **offering enterprise AI solutions rather than just API access, similar to how Microsoft offers AI-powered business tools.**

What's Next for Deepseek?

Deepseek's first models have already shaken the AI industry, but **what comes next?**

1. Expansion Beyond Text Generation:

Currently, Deepseek focuses primarily on **language-based AI** (chatbots, coding, reasoning). However, future versions may expand into:

✓ **Multimodal AI** – Handling **text, images, and video together** like GPT-4o and Gemini.

✓ **AI Agents** – Models that can **autonomously execute tasks** (e.g., AI assistants that browse the web, send emails, or write reports).

✓ **AI-Generated Creativity** – Music, video generation, and advanced AI-generated media.

Prediction: By 2026, Deepseek could **introduce a multimodal model that competes with GPT-4o andGemini1.5.**

2.Improvements in Reasoning & Scientific AI:

Deepseek-R1 already **outperforms GPT-4 in logic-heavy tasks**, but the next frontier in AI development is **scientific AI**, including:

✓ **AI for Mathematics & Theoretical Science** – Helping researchers solve complex problems.

✓ **AI for Medical Research** – Assisting in drug discovery and diagnostics.

✓ **Autonomous AI Decision-Making** – AI that can make informedchoices without human intervention.

Prediction: The next version of Deepseek may **specialize in reasoning-based AI, potentially becoming the best model for scientific applications.**

3. Expanding to Edge AI & Local AI:

Deepseek has already proven that **high-quality AI models can be run on consumer hardware**. In the future, we may see:

✓ **AI running on smartphones & IoT devices** – Eliminating cloud dependence.

✓ **Ultra-low power AI chips** – AI models designed to run without internetaccess.

✓ **Decentralized AI networks** – Models that run across distributed local servers, similar to blockchain technology.

Prediction: By 2027, AI models like Deepseek could be **fully decentralized, running directly on personal devices instead of cloud servers.**

Final Thoughts: The Democratization of AI:

Deepseek's emergence marks a turning point for **AI accessibility, cost efficiency, and global competition**. For years, AI has been dominated by **Silicon Valley**, requiring massive budgets and proprietary technology. However, Deepseek has shown that **high-performance AI can be built affordably, openly, and efficiently.**

What This Means for the AI Industry:

✓ **Startups & Developers** – No longer dependent on **expensive proprietary models like GPT-4.**

✓ **Researchers & Scientists** – Gain access to **state-of-the-art AI without restrictions.**

✓ **Governments & Policymakers** – Need to **adapt to a world where AI is open and decentralized.**

The Big Question: Will AI become **a tool controlled by a few powerful corporations, or will it remain open-source and freely available to all?**

With Deepseek's success, the future of AI may belong **not to the richest companies, but to the most efficient, innovative, and open-minded developers**.

Appendices:

Key AI Terms Explained:

Large Language Model (LLM): A type of AI trained on massive amounts of text data to generate human-like responses.

Transformer Architecture: The neural network structure used in AI models like GPT-4and Deepseek, enabling efficient language processing.

Mixture of Experts (MoE): A technique that activates only certain parts of a model for specific tasks, improving efficiency.

Chain of Thought Reasoning (CoT): A method where AI breaks down complex problems into step-by-step logical reasoning.

Distillation: A process where a larger model is used to train a smaller one, retaining intelligence while reducing computational costs. **Open-Source AI**: AI models whose code and weights are freely available for modification and redistribution.

Comparison Table: Deepseek vs Open AI vs Llama vs Claude

Feature	Deepseek-V3	GPT-4o (OpenAI)	Claude3.5 (Anthropic)	Llama 3 (Meta)
Open-Source	■ Yes	✕ No	✕ No	■ Yes
Training Cost	$5.6M	$100M+	$50M+	$30M+
Math& Logic Performance				
Coding Abilities				
APICost (per Million Tokens)	$0.10	$4.40	$3.00	$0.20
Runs Locally?	✅ Yes	✕ No	✕ No	■ Yes

How to Get Started with Deepseek(Code Examples &API Setup)

Using Deepseek API

Step 1: Get an API Key from the Deepseek website.

Step 2: Install necessary libraries.

Step 3: Make a request to Deepseek's API

Bash
Pip install requests
Python
| ```
import requests
API_KEY="your_deepseek_api_key"url="https://api.deepseek.com /v1/chat" payload =
{ "model": "deepseek-v3",  "messages":
[{"role":"user","content": "What is Deepseek?"} ]
}headers={
"Authorization":f"Bearer{API_KEY}","Content-Type":
"application/json"

 response = requests.post(url, json=payload, headers=headers)
print(response.json())
``` |
```

Running Deepseek Locally

Step1:Install Dependencies

Step 2: Load Deepseek Model

Bash
Pip install torch transformers accelerate
Python
fromtransformersimport AutoModelForCausalLM, Auto Tokenizermodel_name ="*deepseek-ai/deepseek-v3*" *tokenizer* =*AutoTokenizer.from_pretrained(model_name)* *model*=*AutoModelForCausalLM.from_pretrained(model_name)* inputs=tokenizer("ExplainDeepseek AI.", return_tensors="pt") outputs = model.generate(**inputs, max_length=200) *print(tokenizer.decode(outputs[0]))*

Step 3: Optimize for Low-End GPUs

Python
fromtransformersimport BitsAndBytesConfigⱦquantization_config = *BitsAndBytesConfig(* *load_in_8bit=True* *)* *model*= *AutoModelForCausalLM.from_pretrained(*

```
model_name,quantization_config=quantization_config )
```

Conclusion: With just a few lines of code, anyone can **start using Deepseek's AI for free, making it an ideal choice for startups, researchers, and businsses.**

Final Thoughts:

Deepseek has **fundamentally changed the AI industry**, proving that **cost-efficient, high-performance AI models can be developed outside of Silicon Valley**.

What This Means for the Future:

✓ Developersworldwidewillshifttoopen-source AI.

✓ Proprietary AI models will face pressure to become cheaper or open-source.

✓ AI will become more decentralized, with more models running on personal hardware.